Kids Can Draw

MONSTERS

W9-CFL-245

by Philippe Legendre

BERKELEY PUBLIC LIBRARY

Walter Foster

© 2002 Groupe Fleurus-Mame, Paris.
Text on pages 4–24 © 2002 Walter Foster Publishing, Inc. All rights reserved.
Original title *J'apprends à dessiner les monstres,* © 1997 Groupe Fleurus-Mame, Paris.

Attention Parents and Teachers

All children can draw a circle, a square, or a triangle . . . which means that they can also learn to draw a jack-o-lantern, ghost, or space alien! The KIDS CAN DRAW learning method is easy and fun. Children will learn a technique and a vocabulary of shapes that will form the basis for all kinds of drawing.

Pictures are created by combining geometric shapes to form a mass of volumes and surfaces. From this stage, children can give character to their sketches with straight, curved, or broken lines.

With just a few strokes of the pencil, a monstrous scene will appear—and with the addition of color, the picture will be real work of art!

The KIDS CAN DRAW method offers a real apprenticeship in technique and a first look at composition, proportion, shapes, and lines. The simplicity of this method ensures that the pleasure of drawing is always the most important factor.

About Philippe Legendre

French painter, engraver, and illustrator, Philippe Legendre also runs a school of art for children aged 6–14 years. Legendre frequently spends time in schools and has developed this method of learning so that all children can discover the artist within themselves.

Helpful Tips

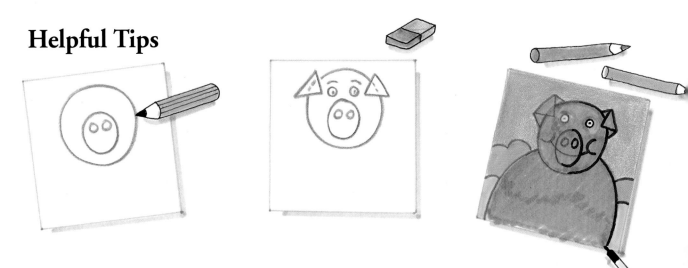

1. Each picture is made up of simple geometric shapes, which are illustrated at the top of the left-hand page. This is called the **Vocabulary of Shapes.** Encourage children to practice drawing each shape before starting their pictures.

2. Suggest children use a pencil to do their sketches. This way, if they don't like a particular shape, they can just erase it and try again.

3. A dotted line indicates that the line should be erased. Have children draw the whole shape and then erase the dotted part of the line.

4. Once children finish their drawings, they can color them with crayons, colored pencils, or felt-tip markers. They may want to go over the lines with a black pencil or pen.

Now let's get started!

This round jack-o-lantern

loves Halloween.

Now color it in

with tangerine.

Jack-o-lantern

Draw three bumps

and then some squiggles.

This ghost shouts, "Boo!"

and then it giggles!

Ghost

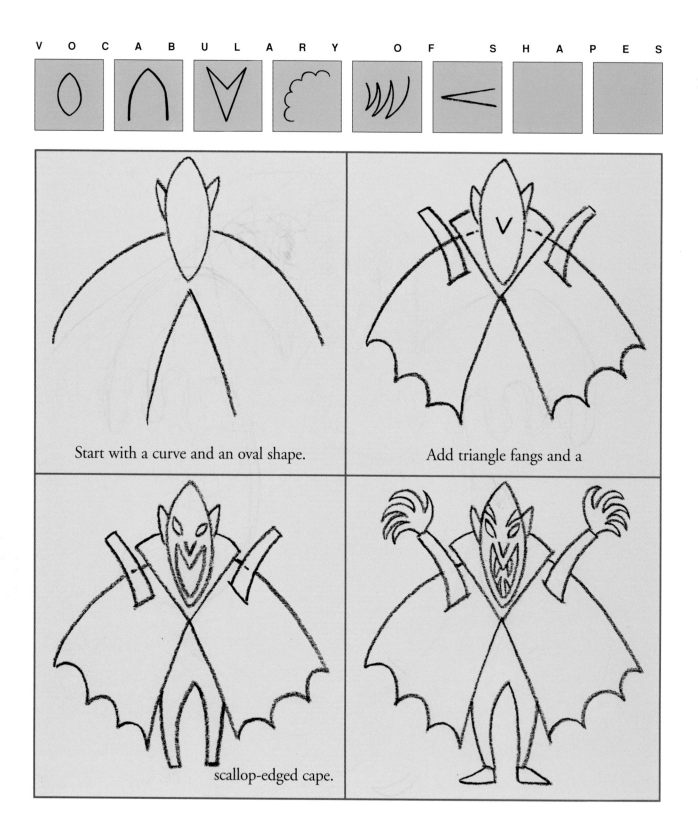

Start with a curve and an oval shape.

Add triangle fangs and a

scallop-edged cape.

Vampire

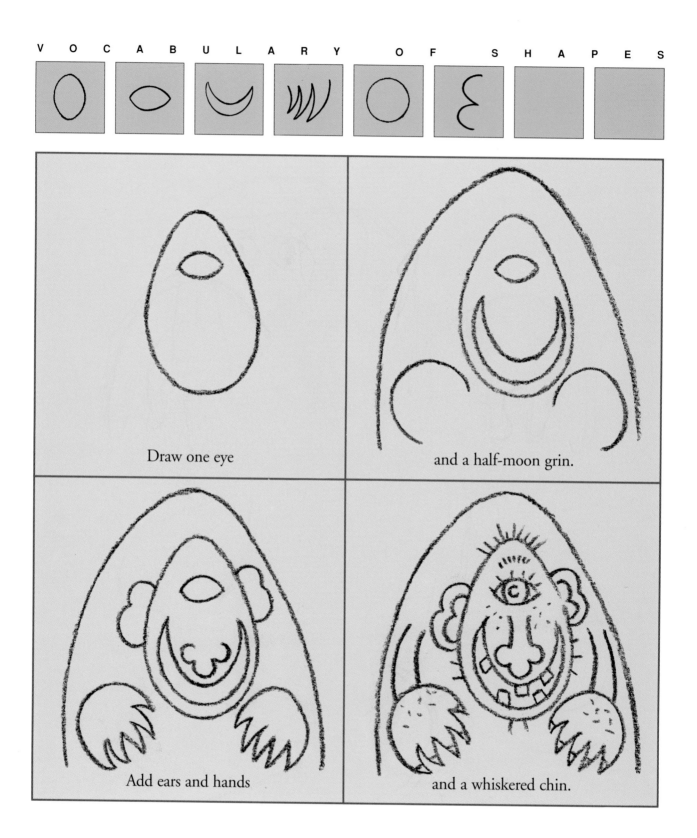

Draw one eye

and a half-moon grin.

Add ears and hands

and a whiskered chin.

Cyclops

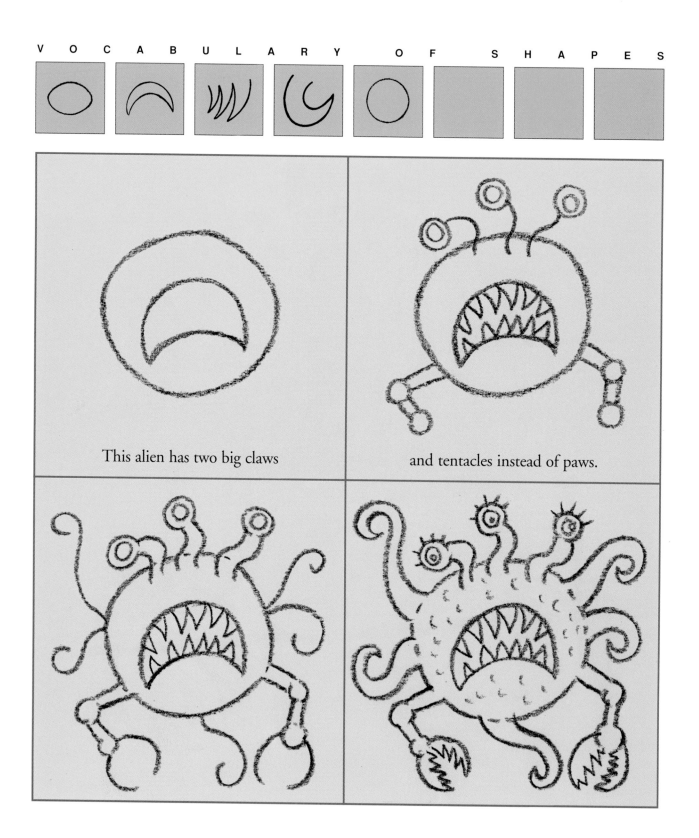

This alien has two big claws

and tentacles instead of paws.

Space Alien

BERKELEY PUBLIC LIBRARY

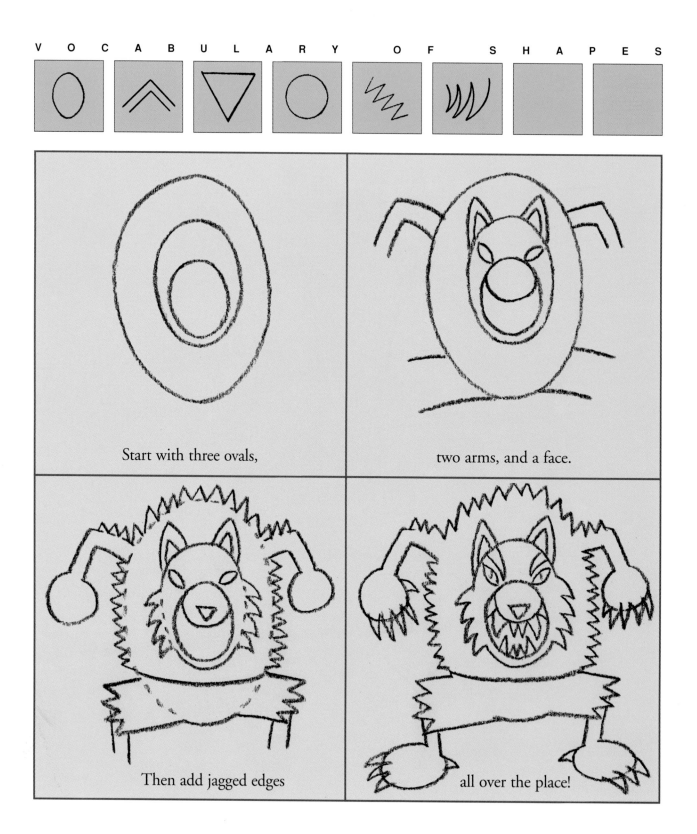

Start with three ovals,

two arms, and a face.

Then add jagged edges

all over the place!

Werewolf

Draw "Mr. Bones"

with a triangle nose,

circles and lines,

and rectangle toes.

Skeleton

From his expression, you can see

that the mad scientist

is not making

tea!

Mad **S**cientist

This little round devil

sure seems to be boasting

his pitchfork is perfect for

marshmallow roasting!

Little Red Devil

They're the silliest monsters that you ever saw!

It's your turn to make them. Now, ready, set—draw!

BERKELEY PUBLIC LIBRARY